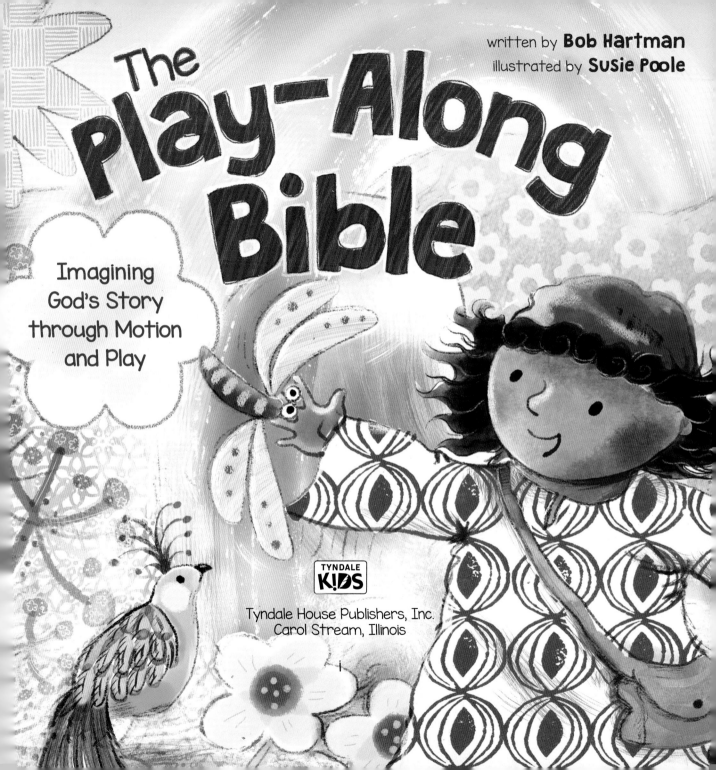

written by **Bob Hartman**
illustrated by **Susie Poole**

The Play-Along Bible

Imagining
God's Story
through Motion
and Play

TYNDALE
K!DS

Tyndale House Publishers, Inc.
Carol Stream, Illinois

i

For Remy

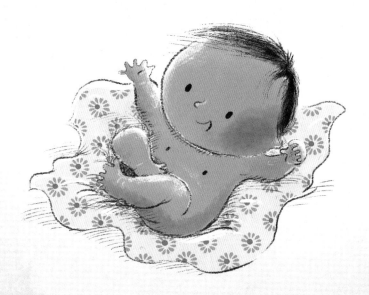

Visit Tyndale's website for kids at www.tyndale.com/kids.

TYNDALE is a registered trademark of Tyndale House Publishers, Inc. The Tyndale Kids logo is a trademark of Tyndale House Publishers, Inc.

Illustrated by Susie Poole

Designed by Jacqueline L. Nuñez

Published in association with the literary agency of William K. Jensen Literary Agency, 119 Bampton Court, Eugene, OR 97404.

For manufacturing information regarding this product, please call 1-800-323-9400.

Library of Congress Cataloging-in-Publication Data

Hartman, Bob, date.
  The play-along Bible : imagining God's story through motion and play / written by Bob Hartman ; illustrated by Susie Poole.
      pages cm
   ISBN 978-1-4964-0864-8 (hc)
1. Bible stories, English. 2. Perceptual-motor learning. I. Poole, Susie, illustrator. II. Title.
   BS551.3.H38 2016
   220.95'05--dc23

                                                                                    2015026382

Printed in China

22	21	20	19	18	17	16
7	6	5	4	3	2	1

Table of Contents

Dear parents and caregivers,

I really enjoyed writing this *Play-Along Bible* for you and your kids. Psalm 78 tells us that we should pass along God's story to our children, and it's my hope that this book will help you do that.

I know that many parents struggle with that idea. They think they don't know enough about the Bible. And they are afraid that telling God's story badly, or in a boring way, might do more harm than good. I have a friend who is a children's pastor. When she was a teenager and babysat for a Christian family, she was told that she could read the children a fun story, but only if she read them a Bible story first! I think that sums up the problem.

My hope is that I have retold these fifty Bible stories in such a way that they actually ARE the fun story. And I have included lots of things for you and your children to do as you read the stories, so that you can all have fun together.

All you need to do is to read each line, and then invite your child to do the suggested action or repeat the suggested words along with you. It's that simple. You may need to go first, to give them an idea of how to do it. And it will help if you do that with a big smile on your face and a playful attitude. Because it is *The Play-Along Bible*, after all. And nearly thirty years of storytelling has convinced me that when we are playing (as opposed to sitting very seriously and still), we are always more open to discovering what is beautiful, good, and true.

We are often told, and I think it's right, that reading to our children from a very young age instills a love of words and a love of books. But I think it does more than that. Lap time, bedtime, class time—whenever you take the time to read to your children not only brings them closer to the words, it also brings them closer to you. So it makes sense, doesn't it, that if the words are about God, then it will surely bring them closer to Him, as well. And what could be better? You and your child and your heavenly Father, all there together, in one place, playing. Playing along with a fun story!

Bob Hartman

Turn On the Lights

Genesis 1:1-5

In the very beginning, everything was completely dark.
You couldn't see a thing. (Place your hands over your eyes. Shut them tight.)
Then God said, "Light!" (Say, "Light!")
And it wasn't dark anymore—it was bright! (Open your eyes.)
God called the light "day" (Shout, "Day!") and the darkness "night."
(Whisper, "Night.")
And that was the first day. (Shout, "Hooray!")

4

Sky High

Genesis 1:6-8

Then God said, "Waters."
(Make a wavy motion with your hands.)
He separated the waters below (Point down.)
and the sky above.
(Point up and draw the shape of a cloud with your finger.)
And that was the second day. (Shout, "Hooray!")

6

Land Ho!

Genesis 1:9-13

Next God said, "Sea," and the waters gathered together.
(Pretend you're swimming.)
Then he said, "Earth," and between the seas rose mountains
(Make the shape of a mountain with your hands.)
and fields (Wave your arms over your head like tall grass.)
and deserts. (Say, "I'm thirsty!")
God said, "Plants!"
And trees and grass and weeds wiggled up out of the ground.
(Wiggle your fingers and toes.)
Then God said, "Fruit." And flowers sprouted from stems,
(Pretend to smell flowers.)
and fruit grew from wavy branches.
(Pretend to take a bite of fruit.)
And that was the third day. (Shout, "Hooray!")

8

Sun, Moon, and Stars— Oh My!

Genesis 1:14-19

Next, God said, "Sun."
(Give a great big sunny smile.)
Then he said, "Moon." (Howl, "Moooooon!")
And he finished by filling the night sky with a shower of shining stars.
(Sing, "Twinkle, Twinkle, Little Star.")
And that was the fourth day. (Shout, "Hooray!")

Splishy Splashy, Squawky Talky

Genesis 1:20-23

Next, God said, "Fish." (Make a fish face!)
And there they were! Loads of sea creatures, splashing and
swimming and doing whatever it is that octopuses do.
(Pretend you're a fish or a crab or an octopus.)
Then God said, "Birds." And they appeared!
Flapping (Flap your arms.)
and chirping (Chirp like a bird.)
and squawking! (Go on—squawk like a parrot!)
And that was the fifth day.
(Shout, "Hooray!")

10

In God's Image

Genesis 1:24-31; 2:4-7, 21-23

God said, "Animals!"
And there were wild animals, (Roar like a lion.)
farm animals, (Moo like a cow.)
and creepy, crawly animals too.
(Move your fingers like a spider.)
Then God said, "People."
And he created a man (Say the name of
a man you know.)
and a woman (Say the name of a woman
you know.)
made in God's image—a little like himself—friends
who could talk with him (Say, "Hello, God!")
and take care of his world. (Make a big circle with your arms.)
And that was the sixth day. (Shout, "Hooray!")

12

14

A Good Rest

Genesis 2:1-3

Then God looked at everything he had made.
"It's all good," he said. (Hold up one thumb.)
"REALLY good!" (Hold up your other thumb.)
And so on the seventh day God did what anyone would do
after six good days of work.
He rested! (Pretend to go to sleep.
Make a little snoring sound.)
And that was the seventh day. (Shout, "Hooray!")

The Sneaky Snake
Genesis 2:15-17; 3:1-24

The first man and the first woman were happy. (Smile.)
REALLY happy. (Smile bigger.)
"Eat any fruit in this beautiful garden," God told them, (Pretend you're gobbling up an apple.)
"EXCEPT the fruit from that one tree, there, in the middle."
(Point and say, "Not that one!")
One day a snake crept up to the woman and told her a lie.
(Wriggle one arm like a snake.)
"There's nothing wrong with eating the fruit from that tree," the snake hissed. (Hiss like a snake.)
What happened next was very sad. (Pretend to cry.)
The man and the woman disobeyed God and ate the fruit! (Gasp!)
So they had to leave the beautiful garden. (Wave good-bye.)

16

Safe from the Storm

Genesis 6:9–8:22

Many years went by, and there were lots more people, but they disobeyed
God too! God was very sad. (Make a sad face.)
But Noah was different. He did what God told him to do. (Give a big hug.)
God helped Noah build a big boat (Pretend you're hammering.)
for his family and two of every kind of animal!
(Make the noise of your favorite animal—twice!)
Then God sent rain. LOTS of rain.
(Pat your legs really fast to make a raining sound.)
Soon the whole world was under water! (Plug your nose.)
But everyone in Noah's boat was safe.
(Wipe your forehead and say, "Whew!")
When the water went down, everyone in the boat stepped
out onto land. (March forward.)
Then God put a rainbow in the sky. (Draw the shape of
a rainbow with your finger.)

18

19

20

A Promise Kept

Genesis 15:1-6; 18:10-15; 21:1-7

Sarah was very old. (Croak, "I'm old.")
Her husband, Abraham, was even older. (Croak, "I'm older.")
They wanted to have children, but they couldn't. (Make a sad face.)
So God gave them a promise. (Cross your heart.)
"I will give you a big family. (Make a big circle with your arms.) More than the
stars in the sky!" (Move your fingers like twinkling stars.)
When Sarah heard this, she laughed. (Laugh.)
But God kept his promise. (Give a thumbs-up.)
Sarah had a baby! (Pretend to rock a baby.)
She called him Isaac, which means "laughter." (Laugh again, louder.)

Jacob's Journey

Genesis 25:19-34; 27:1–33:20

Isaac had two sons—Jacob and Esau. (Hold up two fingers.)
Jacob tricked Esau, (Rub your hands together
and make a sneaky little laugh.)
and that made Esau angry! (Make an angry face.)
So Jacob ran away. (Run in place.)
He stopped to sleep
(Tilt your head and rest it on your hands.)
and dreamed of angels going up and down a
ladder. (Look up. Shout, "Whoa!")
Later, he married the love of his life
(Say, "Aww!")
and even wrestled with God!
(Wrap your arms around yourself
and squeeze.)
Then God sent Jacob home to make peace
with his brother Esau.
(Shake hands with someone.)

23

Joseph's Jealous Brothers

Genesis 37

Jacob had 12 sons, but he loved Joseph the best.
He gave Joseph a beautiful coat. (Put on a pretend coat.)
Joseph had special dreams about the things that would happen to his family.
(Point to your head.)
"You will all bow down to me," he told his brothers. (Bow.)
That made them very angry. (Make an angry face.)
So they sold Joseph as a slave, and he was carried off to the land of Egypt!
(Put your wrists together like they're tied up.)
Then the brothers told a lie to their father, Jacob.
(Hiss like the sneaky snake in the garden.)
"A wild animal killed Joseph!" they said. (Roar like a lion.)
Jacob was very sad. (Pretend to cry.)

26

Off to Prison

Genesis 39-40

Far away from home, Joseph worked as a slave
for an important man named Potiphar. (Salute.)
Joseph was a good worker! He made Potiphar happy.
(Smile wide, and give a thumbs-up.)
But one day that changed. (Say, "Uh-oh.")
Potiphar's wife told a lie about Joseph.
(Hiss like the sneaky snake in the garden.)
"Joseph did something bad!" she said. So Potiphar sent Joseph to prison.
(Pretend you're holding prison bars.)
But God was still with Joseph! (Point up.)
Two prisoners had dreams. (Point to your head.)
And God helped Joseph understand the meanings of their dreams!
(Snap your fingers.)

Pharaoh's Dream

Genesis 41:1-57; 42:1-5; 45:3-11

One night Pharaoh, the king, had a dream.
(Point to your head.)
God helped Joseph explain it. (Snap your fingers.)
There would be seven years with lots of food (Pat your tummy.)
and then seven years with little.
(Make a growling noise like your stomach is rumbling.)
Pharaoh thanked Joseph and set him free!
(Put your wrists together. Now pull them apart!)
He asked Joseph to help everyone save some food.
(Make pretend piles of food.)
Joseph's brothers came from far away asking
for something to eat. (Cup your hands together.)
When they saw Joseph, they were very surprised and thought
he would be angry. (Shake like you're scared.)
But Joseph forgave them!
(Give a hug.)

28

29

River Baby

Exodus 2:1-10

There was a basket floating in the river.
(Sit down and rock back and forth.)
Inside was a baby boy!
(Make a surprised face.)
The baby's big sister was watching him
from a distance,
(Pretend you're peeking through some bushes.)
and God was watching too.
Pharaoh's daughter found the basket
and heard the baby boy crying. (Cry, "Waa!")
She needed someone to help care for the baby.
(Pretend to give the baby a kiss.)
The baby's sister popped out (Jump up.)
and shouted, "I know someone!" (Hold one finger in the air.)
So the baby's own mother helped take care of him, and Pharaoh's daughter
named him Moses. (Pretend to rock a baby.)

30

31

A Bush on Fire

Exodus 1:8-14; 2:11-15; 3:1-10

Moses grew up in the house of Pharaoh,
the king of Egypt.
(Make the shape of a house
with your hands.)
But Moses' mother and father
were part of
Jacob's family, called the Hebrews—
God's people! (Point up.)
Pharaoh had made the Hebrews his slaves.
(Put your wrists together like they're tied up.)
When Moses grew up,
(Raise your hands up, up, up.)
God talked to him in the desert from a burning bush!
(Say, "Whoosh!")
God said, "Tell Pharaoh to set my people free!"
(Cross your hands. Then pull them apart.)

32

"Let God's People Go!"

Exodus 5-14

Moses told Pharaoh, "Let God's people go!" (Cross your hands. Then pull them apart.)
But Pharaoh wouldn't listen. (Cover your ears.)
So God sent flies, (Swat the air.)
hail, (Duck and cover your head!)
locusts, (Hop around.)
and other bad things that made life hard for the Egyptians. (Wipe your forehead.)
Finally Pharaoh said, "Go!" (Point and say, "Go!")
So God's people left! (Wave good-bye.)
Then Pharaoh changed his mind. (Point to your head.)
He sent soldiers in chariots to stop them. (Pretend to ride a chariot.)
But God split the Red Sea in two (Put your hands together.
Then spread them far apart.)
and his people got away! (Shout, "Hooray!")

·36·

Big Wall, Big Fall

Joshua 1:1-9; 6:1-20

Once God's people were free, (Cross your hands. Then pull them apart.)
he led them in the wilderness until they reached the land
he had promised them. (Cross your heart.)
God told their new leader, Joshua, to be brave and strong. (Flex your muscles.)
They came to a city called Jericho, which had tall walls. (Look waaaaay up.)
"For six days," God told Joshua,
"march one time around the city." (March in place.)
"On day seven," God said, "march around the city seven times."
(March and count out seven steps.)
So they obeyed God. Then they blew trumpets (Make a trumpeting sound.)
and shouted. (Cup your hands around your mouth and shout, "Fall down!")
And the walls fell down! (Shout, "Boom!")

A New Start

Ruth 1-4

Poor Naomi! First her husband died.
(Make a sad face.)
Then her two sons died.
(Rub your eyes and pretend to cry.)
She wanted to go back to her home.
(Walk slowly in place.)
So Ruth, her son's wife, said she would
go too. (Hold hands with someone.)
When they got there, Ruth worked
in the fields, gathering grain,
so they would have food to eat.
(Pretend to pick up grain
off the ground.)
A man named Boaz saw Ruth.
(Point to your eyes.)
Boaz obeyed God's law
and helped Ruth and Naomi.
And later he even became Ruth's husband.
(Pretend to give a big, smoochy kiss.)

38

Hearing God's Voice

1 Samuel 3:1-11

Three times Samuel woke up when he heard somebody call his name.
(Say, "Samuel" three times.)
Three times he got out of bed. (Lie down. Then stand up again.)
Three times he woke up Eli, the priest.
(Gently shake the person next to you and whisper, "Wake up.")
"It must be God calling you," Eli finally said. "Next time, say,
'I'm listening, Lord.'" (Put your hand to your ear.)
So Samuel did. (Say, "I'm listening, Lord.")
And God spoke to him.
So Samuel listened to God and, for the rest of his life,
told people the messages God gave him. (Put your hand to your ear again.)

41

42

David Saves the Day

I Samuel 17:1-54

Goliath was a scary giant. He was nine feet tall!
(Raise your hands above your head.)
He was mean to God's people and
said bad things about God. (Say, "Oh no!")
"Send someone to fight me!" he shouted.
(Shake your fist.)
"If I win, you must be our slaves!"
(Cross your wrists.)
All of God's people were afraid.
(Tremble and make a scared face.)
But David trusted God. He wasn't afraid.
(Make a tough face.)
David put a stone in his sling.
(Pretend to pick up a stone.)
He spun it around
(Spin your hand over your head.)
and let it fly. (Say, "Whoosh!")
The stone hit the giant on the head.
(Poke your forehead with your finger.)
And God's people were saved! (Shout, "Hooray!")

43

A Fishy Situation

Jonah 1:1–3:10

"Go to the city of Nineveh," God told Jonah.
(Point your finger and say, "Go.")
"Tell the people there to change their bad ways."
(Shake your finger like you're scolding someone.)
But Jonah didn't want to go. (Shake your head and say, "No.")
So he got on a ship and went the other way. (Point behind you.)
But God sent a storm, (Say, "Boom!" like thunder.)
and Jonah ended up in the sea. (Pretend you are sinking in water.)
So God sent a fish to swallow Jonah (Say, "Gulp!")
and spit him back on the land. (Say, "Ptooey!")
Then Jonah obeyed God (Point forward
and nod your head.)
and went to Nineveh. (Start walking.)
The people there heard God's message,
(Put your hand to your ear.)
and they changed their bad ways.
(Shout, "Hooray!")

44

Cool in the Furnace

Daniel 3:1-28

King Nebuchadnezzar told everyone to bow down to a statue.
(Freeze like a statue.)
Shadrach, Meshach, and Abednego knew that would be wrong.
(Slowly shake your head.)
"We will only bow down to God and serve him," they told the king. (Point up.)
The king was so angry, he threw them into a fiery furnace! (Shout, "Hot!")
But God sent an angel to protect them. (Hold your arms out like a shield.)
And they were not burned at all. (Say, "Not hot!")
So King Nebuchadnezzar brought them out of the furnace (Say, "Whew!")
and praised God too! (Bow down.)

The Lions Stay Hungry

Daniel 6:1-28

The hungry lions roared. (Roar like a lion!)
Poor Daniel was in the lions' den (Say, "Oh no!")
because he had prayed to God (Fold your hands in prayer)
even though King Darius said not to.
(Shake your head.)
But Daniel knew he had to obey God.
(Fold your hands in prayer again.)
So God sent an angel to shut
the lions' mouths.
(Hold your lips shut with your fingers.)
The king saw that God had
saved Daniel.
So he praised God too.
(Shout, "Yay, God!")

A Special Message
Matthew 1:18-24; Luke 1:26-38

The angel Gabriel went to see Mary. (Make a surprised face.)
"God wants to give you a special baby!" he told her. (Pretend to rock a baby.)
"The baby will be God's own Son, Jesus."
Mary didn't understand, (Shrug your shoulders.)
but she still obeyed God. (Nod your head.)
Mary was supposed to get married to a man named Joseph.
He didn't understand either! (Make a confused face.)
So God's angel visited him, too. (Make a surprised face.)
"Mary's telling the truth," the angel said. (Cross your heart.)
"She will have a baby—God's own Son!" (Point up.)
"Okay," said Joseph. "I will not be afraid! I will marry her after all. And Mary
will be my wife!" (Make kissy sounds.)

Away in a Manger

Luke 2:1-7

Mary and Joseph went on a trip. (Walk in place.)
It was a very long way. (Walk slowly.)
Finally they came to Bethlehem, and soon it was time for Mary to have her baby. (Make baby noises.)
But there was no space for them! Bethlehem was crowded. (Press yourself right up next to somebody.)
So Mary and Joseph stayed with the animals. (Make barn animal sounds.)
And that's where God's Son, Jesus, was born. (Pretend to rock a baby.)

52

53

The Savior Has Been Born!

Luke 2:8-20

Near Bethlehem, shepherds were
watching their sheep. (Say, "Baaaa.")
An angel came to give them
a message. (Make a surprised face.)
"Good news!" he said.
(Give a thumbs-up.)
"God has sent someone to save you."
(Shout, "Hooray!")
"He's in Bethlehem—a baby, lying in a manger."
(Pretend to rock a baby.)
Then more angels arrived
(Flap your arms like the wings of an angel.)
praising God. (Sing a Christmas song,
like "Joy to the World.")
Then they disappeared, and the shepherds hurried off to find baby Jesus.
(Put your hand above your eyes, looking.)

New Star, New King

Matthew 2:1-12

After Jesus was born, a special star appeared.
(Move your fingers like twinkling stars.)
"It means God's people have a new king," some wise men said.
(Pretend to put a crown on your head.)
"Let's go see the new king."
(Snap your fingers.)
They went a long way to look for him.
(Pretend you're riding a camel.)
Finally the star led them to a house.
They were so happy! (Smile big!)
When they found Jesus, they bowed down (Bow down.)
and gave him presents. (Hold out your arms.)
Jesus was the new king! (Say, "Long live the king!")

57

Where Is Jesus?

Luke 2:41-52

When Jesus was 12 years old, he went to a festival in Jerusalem—God's special city. (Look around, point, and say, "Wow!")

On the way home, Mary and Joseph couldn't find Jesus.
(Say, "Where are you?")

They looked everywhere.
(Put your hand above your eyes, looking.)

Finally they found him! (Say, "Whew.")

He was talking with some teachers in the Temple, God's house. (Make each hand into a puppet, like they're talking to each other.)

"You didn't have to worry," Jesus said to Mary and Joseph. (Give a worried look.)

"I was here, in my Father's house!" (Point up.)

59

Someone Special

Matthew 3:1-17; John 1:29-31

Jesus' cousin John lived in the desert. (Hoot like an owl.)
He ate honey (Say, "Yum.")
and locusts. (Say, "Yuck.")
"God is sending someone very special,"
John told the people. (Give a thumbs-up.)
"So say you're sorry,
and stop doing bad things." (Say, "I'm sorry.")
Then Jesus came to see John.
Jesus was all grown up! (Look up.)
"Jesus is the one I told you about!"
John said to the people. (Clap your hands.)
When John baptized Jesus,
a dove came down from the sky. (Coo like a dove.)
Then God said to Jesus, "You're my Son,
and I'm very proud of you." (Give a hug.)

Fishing for People!

Luke 5:1-11

"Keep fishing," Jesus said to Peter.
(Pretend you're throwing a net into the water.)
"We fished all night," Peter replied, (Yawn.)
"and we didn't catch a thing."
(Hold out your empty hands.)
But Peter obeyed Jesus anyway and
threw out his nets.
(Throw the net again.)
Soon they were full of fish!
(Make a fish face.)
Peter's friends came over to help.
(Pretend you're rowing a boat.)
The fish filled up their boat too.
(Say, "Wow!")
"Follow me," Jesus said,
"and we'll go fishing for people."
(Pretend to throw a net
in the water again.)

62

Through the Roof

Mark 2:1-12

The house was full. (Squish up next to someone.)
Lots of people were listening to Jesus. (Cup your hand to your ear.)
One man wanted to get to Jesus, but he couldn't walk. (Sit down.)
So four of his friends carried him. (Pretend to lift something heavy.)
But they couldn't get in the house. So they brought him
onto the roof and made a hole. (Pretend to dig.)
They lowered their friend into the house.
(Make a surprised face.)
Jesus forgave all the bad things the man had done
(Shout, "I'm forgiven!") and then healed him.
(Shout, "I can walk!")

65

A Soldier's Trust

Matthew 8:5-13

A Roman soldier's servant was very sick. (Say, "I don't feel very well.")
Some Romans were mean, (Pretend to wave a sword.)
but not this one. (Put away the sword.)
"I'm powerful!" the soldier said. (Make a muscle with one arm.)
"And so are you, Jesus. (Make a muscle with your other arm.)
My servant will get better if you just say so."
Jesus was surprised that the soldier trusted him this much.
(Make a surprised face.)
"Go home," Jesus told him. "Because you believed,
I will heal your servant." (Say, "Be healed.")
And right away, the servant felt better! (Shout, "Hooray!")

67

No More Storm

Matthew 8:23-27

Jesus and his friends
were riding in a boat. (Say, "Yo-ho!")
The waves rocked the boat gently.
(Rock back and forth gently.)
Jesus fell asleep. (Shut your eyes and snore.)
Then the wind blew hard (Take a deep breath
and blow it out like a strong wind!)
and the waves crashed.
(Rock back and forth faster.)
Jesus' friends were scared.
(Shout, "Wake up, Jesus!")
So Jesus shushed the wind
(Say, "Wind, shhh!")
and told the waves to be still.
(Stand very still.)
And everyone was safe.
(Rock back and forth gently.)

69

Just Have Faith

Mark 5:21-24, 35-43

A little girl was very sick.
(Say, "I don't feel very well.")
So Jairus, her father, asked Jesus to come to his house and heal her.
(Kneel down and say, "Please!")
On the way there, the man's friends came and said,
"We're sorry. Your daughter died." (Say, "Oh no!")
"Don't worry," Jesus said. "Just trust me."
Jesus went inside the house.
"She's only sleeping," he said. (Close your eyes.)
Some people laughed at that. (Laugh.)
But Jesus went to where the girl was lying.
(Lie down on the floor.)
He took the girl's hand. "Get up!" he said.
And she did! (Stand up and cheer!)

The Huge Feast

John 6:1-13

Lots and lots and LOTS of people came looking for Jesus.
(Put your hand above your eyes, looking.)
They were really hungry.
(Make a growling noise like your stomach is rumbling.)
So a boy with two fish (Hold up two fingers.)
and five loaves of bread (Hold up five fingers.)
gave Jesus his lunch. (Hold out your hands.)
Jesus prayed and thanked God. (Bow your head.)
When he passed out the bread and fish,
(Pretend you're handing out food.)
there was enough food for everyone!
(Say, "Yum!" and hold your belly like you're full.)

A Walk on the Water

Matthew 14:22-33

Jesus' friends were in a boat again. (Rock back and forth gently.)
Suddenly, the wind blew hard. (Take a deep breath
and blow it out like a strong wind!)
The waves crashed! (Say, "Whoosh!")
They thought they saw a ghost. (Point across the room and gasp!)
But it was Jesus, walking on the water! (Say, "WOW!")
Peter said, "If it's really you, Jesus,
ask me to come join you." (Say, "Can I come too?")
"Come on, then!" Jesus said. (Wave your arm.)
So Peter walked on the water too! (Say, "WOW!")
But the wind and waves scared him,
and he started to sink! (Pretend to sink.)
So Jesus reached out and helped Peter
back into the boat.
(Wipe your forehead. Say, "Whew!")

Runaway Sheep

Luke 15:1-7

A shepherd had 100 sheep. (Say, "Baaaa.")
But one sheep wandered away. (Bleat, "I'm lost.")
So the shepherd left the other sheep (Wave good-bye.)
and went to look for his lost sheep.
(Put your hand above your eyes, looking.)
He looked high (Look up.)
and low (Look down.)
and all around. (Look all around.)
Finally he found her!
(Point and say, "There you are!")
So the shepherd took the sheep home
(Bleat, "I'm baaaack!")
and threw a big party. (Do a happy dance.)

Keep Searching

Luke 15:8-10

A woman had 10 silver coins. (Hold up 10 fingers.)
But one coin rolled away. (Say, "It's lost!")
So she lit her lamp (Pretend to strike a match.)
and swept her floor (Make a sweeping motion.)
and looked high (Look up.)
and low (Look down.)
and all around. (Look all around.)
And finally she found her coin! (Shout, "Hooray!")
So she threw a party and invited her neighbors and friends!
(Do a happy dance.)

A Good Neighbor

Luke 10:30-37

A man was walking down the road (Walk forward.)
when something bad happened. (Say, "Oh no!")
Robbers beat him up and took everything he had. (Say, "Ouch!")
They left him hurt on the road. (Pretend to cry.)
A priest walked by (Walk in place.) but did not help him. (Shake your head.)
A Temple worker walked by, (Walk in place.) but he didn't help either!
(Shake your head.)
Then one of the man's enemies walked by. (Walk in place.)
He felt sorry for the man and helped him get better.
(Pretend to stick a bandage on your arm.)
He was a good neighbor! (Give a hug.)

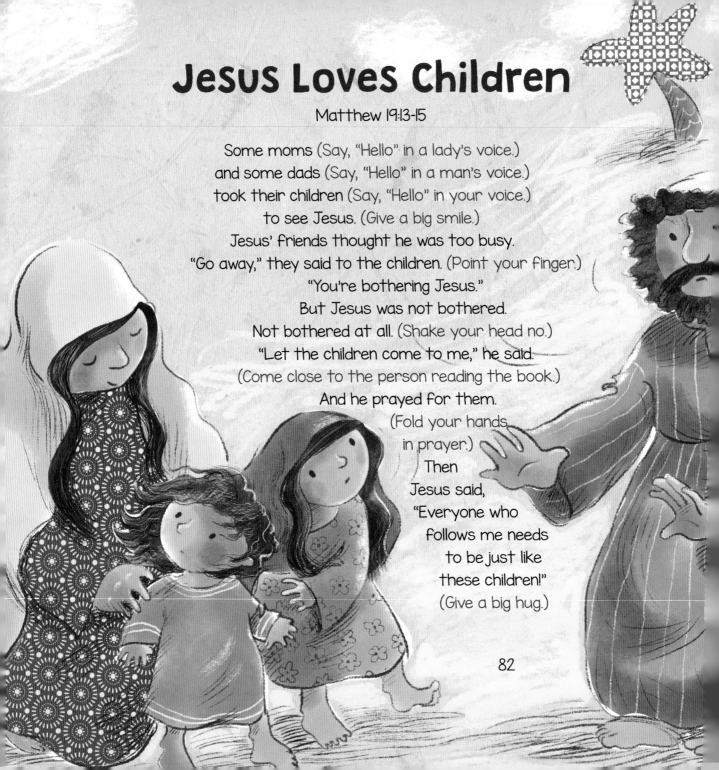

Jesus Loves Children

Matthew 19:13-15

Some moms (Say, "Hello" in a lady's voice.)
and some dads (Say, "Hello" in a man's voice.)
took their children (Say, "Hello" in your voice.)
to see Jesus. (Give a big smile.)
Jesus' friends thought he was too busy.
"Go away," they said to the children. (Point your finger.)
"You're bothering Jesus."
But Jesus was not bothered.
Not bothered at all. (Shake your head no.)
"Let the children come to me," he said.
(Come close to the person reading the book.)
And he prayed for them.
(Fold your hands in prayer.)
Then Jesus said, "Everyone who follows me needs to be just like these children!"
(Give a big hug.)

82

Up a Tree

Luke 19:1-10

Nobody liked Zacchaeus, the tax collector. (Make a mean face.)
He cheated people and took their money.
(Pretend to pull some coins out of a pocket.)
But when Jesus came to town, (Smile and wave.)
Zacchaeus wanted to see him. (Put your hand above your eyes, looking.)
Since Zacchaeus was short, he climbed up a tree
to watch for Jesus. (Pretend to climb.)
When Jesus passed by, he saw Zacchaeus and said,
"Come down! (Wave your arm.) I want to go to your house today."
So they talked and ate together. (Pretend to eat.)
And Zacchaeus changed his bad ways! (Say, "That's better.")

Clippity-Clop

Matthew 21:1-11

"Bring me a donkey to ride on," Jesus told his friends. (Say, "Hee-haw.")
He told them where they could find one.
So his friends brought him a donkey. (Pretend you're scratching
a donkey's head.)
Jesus climbed on the donkey's back
(Say, "Hee-haw!")
and rode down the hill into Jerusalem.
(Say, "Clippity-clop. Clippity-clop.")
People laid palm branches on the road
in front of the donkey. (Pretend to lay down
palm branches. Say, "Hee-haw!")
They praised God and shouted,
"Hosanna!" and "Hooray for God's King!"
(Shout, "Hosanna!")

Who Gave the Most?

Mark 12:41-44

Jesus was at the Temple in Jerusalem. (Fold your hands in prayer.)
He watched people give their money to God.
(Pretend you're holding out some money.)
They dropped their coins into a box. (Say, "Jingle jangle.")
Rich people gave lots of money. (Shout, "JINGLE JANGLE!")
Everyone was impressed. (Say, "Ooh. Aah!")
But a poor woman who had only two coins (Hold up two fingers.)
put both of her coins into the box. (Whisper, "Clink, clink.")
"That woman gave the most," Jesus said,
"because she gave everything she had."
(Hold out your empty hands.)

89

The Cross

Luke 23:26-46

Jesus did many good things!
He healed sick people, (Say, "I feel better.")
and he taught people about God's love.
(Make the shape of a heart with your hands.)
But some people didn't like Jesus. (Make an angry face.)
So they arrested him (Cross your wrists like they're tied up.)
and put him on a cross. (Hold up your arms in the shape of a cross.)
But he still showed God's love (Give a big hug.)
and forgave the people who put him there. (Say, "Wow!")
Then, when his good work was done, he died there on the cross.
(Make a sad face.)
He died to take away all the bad things that people do
(Pretend you are erasing something.)
and to help us do the things we should do too.
(Say, "Thank you, Jesus!")

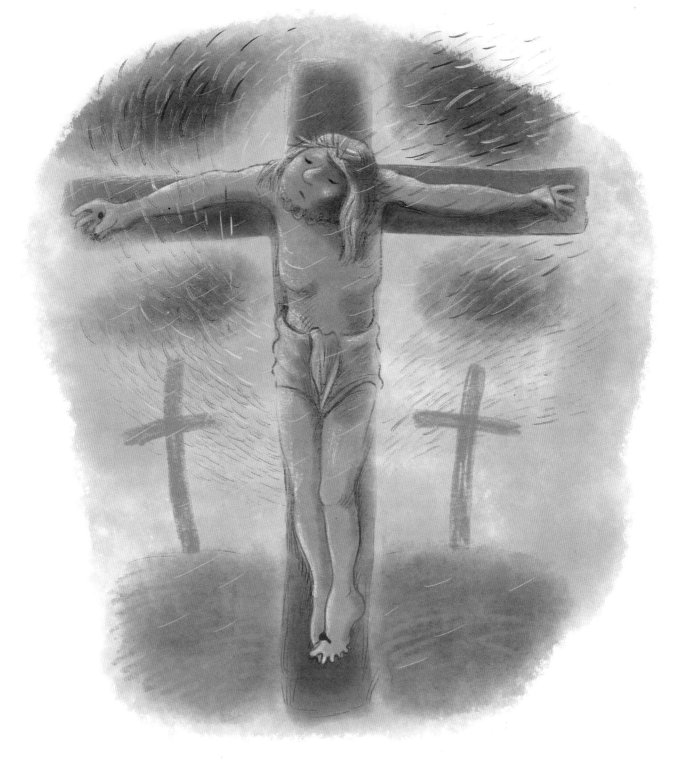

Alive Again!

Matthew 28:1-10

Three days after Jesus died, some women who were friends
of Jesus went to visit his tomb. (Make a sad face.)
Suddenly there was an earthquake! (Shake your whole body!)
An angel came down from heaven (Point up.)
and rolled away the stone that blocked the tomb.
(Pretend to push a heavy stone.)
"Jesus is alive!" the angel said. (Shout, "Wow!")
The women ran to tell the rest of Jesus' friends.
(Run in place and smile big!)
And along the way, they met Jesus!
(Shout, "Hooray!")

Good-bye, Jesus!

Luke 24:42-43; John 20:19; I Corinthians 15:6; Acts 1:6-12

Jesus had a special body after he came back to life.
(Touch your arms and face.)
He could eat and drink like you and me. (Make a sound like you're eating.)
But he could also appear behind locked doors! (Make a surprised face.)
For 40 days he visited lots of his friends. (Say, "Hi!")
Then, one day, he took his friends to a mountain.
(Make the shape of a mountain with your hands.)
"Tell everyone in the world about me," he said.
(Cup your hands around your mouth.)
Then Jesus said good-bye. He went up into the sky
and disappeared in a cloud.
(Wave. Say, "Good-bye, Jesus!")

94

95.

The Holy Spirit Comes

Acts 1:4-8; 2:1-41

Jesus didn't want his friends to feel sad and alone. (Make a sad face.)
So after Jesus went to heaven, (Look up.)
he sent them his Holy Spirit.
His friends were all together when suddenly they heard a rushing wind!
(Take a deep breath and blow it out like the wind!)
Then something that looked like fire rested on each of them.
(Say, "Whoosh!")
And they could speak in different languages that they had never learned!
(Say, "Bonjour! Ni hao!")
Soon other people heard the noise and came running. (Run in place.)
Peter told them about Jesus and the Holy Spirit.
And lots of people believed! (Shout, "Hooray!")

Seeing the Light

Acts 22:1-21

Lots of people believed in Jesus. (Say, "I believe!")
But Saul didn't like that. (Make a grumpy face and say, "I'm Saul.")
He put them in jail. (Pretend you're holding prison bars.)
One day, as Saul was walking down the road, he was blinded by a bright light.
(Cover your eyes with your hands.)
It was Jesus! "Why are you fighting against me?" Jesus asked. (Say, "Why?")
Then Saul believed in Jesus. (Point to your heart.)
After Saul could see again, (Cover your eyes. Then open them!)
he started following Jesus (March in place.)
and telling everyone about him.
(Cup your hands around your mouth.)
Instead of hurting Jesus' followers, he helped them. (Shout, "Yay!")
His life changed so much that, later,
he even went by a new name—Paul. (Smile and say, "I'm Paul.")

100

Starting Anew

Revelation 21:1-7

John, one of Jesus' friends, got to see what God
has planned (Point to your eyes.)
for the future. (Point ahead.)
God will make a new heaven (Look up.)
and a new earth. (Make a circle with your arms.)
There will be no more tears (Pretend to wipe away a tear.)
or pain (Say, "Ouch.")
or dying. (Make a sad face.)
God will be there with us (Give a big hug.)
forever! (Shout, "Hooray!")

Special Bible Verses to Remember

In the beginning God created the heavens and the earth.
Genesis 1:1

The LORD is my shepherd; I have all that I need.
Psalm 23:1

Love your neighbor as yourself.
Matthew 22:39

I can do everything through Christ, who gives me strength.
Philippians 4:13